Pot Pourri:

A KALEIDOSCOPE OF EMOTIONS AND EXPERIENCES

Madhu Goyle

BlueRose ONE.com
Stories Matter
NewDelhi • London

BLUEROSE PUBLISHERS
India | U.K.

For permissions requests or inquiries regarding this publication, please contact:

BLUEROSE PUBLISHERS
www.BlueRoseONE.com
info@bluerosepublishers.com
+91 8882 898 898
+4407342408967

ISBN: 978-93-6452-414-8

Cover design: Daksh
Typesetting: Tanya Raj Upadhyay

First Edition: January 2025

Dedicated to my mother

Mother

Dear Mummy, how I really miss you
And in a moment of quietude, shed a tear or two
In my fond remembrance of you.

You were the epitome of love and grace
And it reflected always on your face
Your finger licking food
Really had us so hooked

You lived to a grand age of Ninety five
With a spirit of ' Never say die '.
Always cheerful and happy
With hands that were forever helping

A leaf or two, we could all borrow from you.
You were the sunshine when our days were gloomy
And the umbrella when they were rainy.

A pillar of strength in our moments of distress
Always ready with your warm embrace.
And forever you will remain our guiding force and light
During the day and in the darkness of night.

Table of Contents

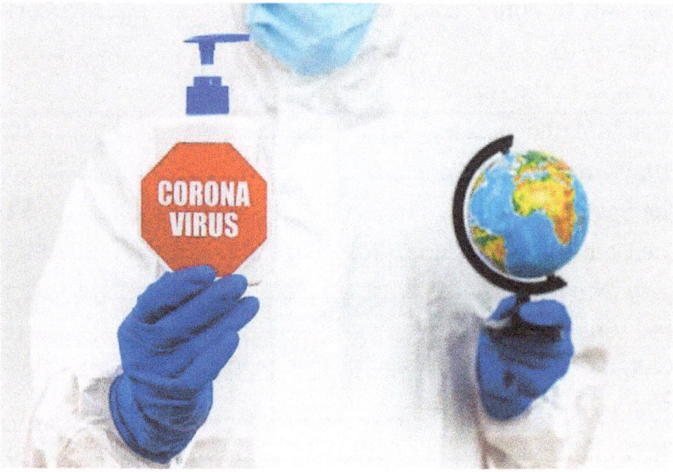
CORONA
VIRUS

Invasion

The silent enemy descended upon us
like an unwanted guest
Putting our limitless freedom to test

It spread its tentacles in a vicious grip
Sending us on an unprecedented fearful
trip

One by one the countries succumbed and fell prey
As it held them in its deadly sway

Oh foolish mankind...!
We had begun to think we were invincible
All it required was a tiny virus to show that we were so vulnerable

It's high time we give up our selfish ways
So that we can hold forth and not go astray

For we need to maintain the balance in nature
And also realise that earth is home to other creatures

So let us join our hands in solidarity
To rise like a phoenix and change our destiny.

Under the Tuscan Sun

I want to indulge in a bit of idleness
To drive away some of my glumness
I want to feel footloose and fancy free
And prance around Citrus laden trees.
Or run across carefully manicured vineyards
And bite into bunches of grapes freshly plucked.
Letting the juice trickle down my face and hands
And feel a little intoxicated with madness.
As if...'Of Opium I had drunk '
Whilst soaking in the Tuscan sun.
A bit of sashaying down the narrow lanes of Florence
To feel the passion of art and artists and their presence
Of a bygone Renaissance world
I have heard and read about so much
And submerge myself in the warm embrace
Of an era of unsullied charm and grace.

My Tryst

With a book in hand and a cup of tea
And the company of the happy busy bees
I made my way in ease
Towards my oasis of peace
When suddenly the bird bath came aflutter
With my sweet, little winged friends of feather
As they tweeted and pecked at the water
And somersaulted in delight and scampered
And beckoned to their mates to gather.
What a heavenly sight to behold
As if I was included in their fold !!
My book went for a toss
Of words.. I was at a loss
As I watched in glee
Their playful soiree.
Can there be a better therapy
Than this, for soothing the mind
And helping the nerves unwind ?

To Live or not to....

For far too long have my wings been clipped
And in a gilded cage have I lived
Now I am too shy
And I don't know how to fly
But I still want to laugh and live a little
And I don't want my life to be brittle
I want to feel free and do as I please
Because I know my time is on lease.

I want to paint the skies with the stories
Of my colourful dreams and fantasies
Whilst riding high above the clouds
On a mystical magical journey
And tell everyone out there to do likewise
Before time runs out and we get diseased.

Love is a game of give and take
But I want to feel its warmth all the same
I want to see all the goodness that resides in people
That makes all our joys become double
And there is still so much light in this world to see
Before darkness finally envelopes me.

My Flight

I wish I could fly
And soar up high
like a bird in the sky
With my wings spread wide
Gliding with ease
As if in peace
Savouring every moment
Of my victorious flight
Feeling so featherless and light
And wander away to an unknown destination
In my heady sensation
Where I could fantasize
Of an Utopian paradise
Away from the self centredness
Of human minds and their selfishness
Love and harmony is all I need
For my eternal existence.

The Lady in White

She floated into my sight
An apparition in white.
A vision so ethereal and spirit like
Silhouetted in the moonlit night.
Mesmerized, I held my breath so tight;
As she sauntered along the beach
So within my reach.
Her gaze upon me she set
And my eyes with hers.. met.
An innocence so endearing,
Which I found so appealing.
Then she swayed;
And her steps faltered.
But before I could get spurred,
She slumped forward.
And on the sand she collapsed..

Sands of Time

I can hear the waves
Softly crashing in the distance
Bathing me in their soothing music
I can hear the seagulls
Calling out to me
Beckoning me to join them
In their flight to freedom.
My mind harks back in time
To bygone, hassle free days
Not a care in the world
All fun and play
But where have they all gone?
Have I changed?
Or has my life slipped away
Like sifting sand
Out of my hands
Nothing in my control
Can I still have hope ?

Spring is in the Air

The wind whispered to the leaves
And they gently swayed and heaved
Happy to be back where they belonged
On the trees in every shade of green.

Their life had been sucked
In the harsh winter months
But it was springtime once more
And the birds were back home
Their endless chirping filled the air
And there was joy and cheer everywhere.

The squirrels, in playful pairs
Up and down the trees went darting
The shy Bunnies with their little pink noses twitching
In and out of the bushes went hopping.

And whilst the bees were merry and humming
Colourful butterflies silently whizzed about kissing and flirting
With the Zinnias and Hydrangeas and Carnations.

The whole place was abuzz with a riot of colours
And I let all these happy sounds and sights of nature
Seep into my bones as I lay on my recliner.

Seaside Wonder

A sky so clear and oh...so very blue !
And the ocean reflecting its every hue..
The soft tawny sand beneath my feet
As I sat on the golden beach in total peace

It felt soothing to be in this far off place
With the gentle breeze softly caressing my face...
And the waves enveloping me in their sweet serenade
Whilst the sparkling blue waters stretched beyond my gaze

Engulfing me in its vast splendour
And enticing me to surrender
To a Bonhomie with the grand Universe...
As it drenched me in its sublime grandeur

Plunging me into the depths of its serenity
Whilst casting an enchanting spell on me
And ushering me into an everlasting camaraderie
As I embarked on an endless journey
Of hope and self discovery
Making me feel so aligned with eternity
With only the cry of an occasional seagull
Breaking my reverie....!!

The Voyage

We set sail on a calm and balmy night
The waves gently lapping against the ship's sides.
The radiant moon beamed down upon us with her silvery eyes
Bidding us a safe passage to the South China isles.

I was a young and newly wedded bride
Of forty days and forty nights
And the Chief Engineer 's wife.
My excitement and euphoria I couldn't hide
As all my story book adventures were coming to life.

I was revelling in the joy of my maiden voyage
As the ship chugged ahead and made good mileage.
We had sailed for twenty four hours and nigh
When the wind suddenly howled and the waves leapt high
And the ship listed from side to side.

My childlike wonder turned to dismay and horror
As nature unleashed it's wrath and terror
Lightning flashed and there was torrential rain and thunder
The ship rocked and rolled out of control
And I had dreadful visions of being washed ashore

The life jackets were ordered to be worn
As we waited fervently for a new morn

And prayed in earnest for the storm to clear
So that we could sail on without any fear
A torturous night we did spend
And none of us slept

But thankfully, God's mercy was bestowed upon us
And we were released from the curse.
As the morning sun pierced through the sky
We realised that we were not going to die.
What a relief it was, just to be alive
And counted our blessings that we were all fine.

The Sparrow

Evenings fall early on days...wintery
When it's cold and dull and dreary.
The trees have become all bare
With no leaves to spare.
Stripped of their verdant glory
They now stand stark and spiky.
The birds have all swarmed
To shores of climate warm.
But from the bushes near...I hear
The tweet of a Sparrow lone
Shriveled and shivering in the cold.
Trying to make a nest she struggles
For her little fledglings to snuggle.
It's true..A Mother's love knows no bounds
And all she cares about is her young ones around.

The Game of life

We are all pawns in the chessboard of life;
There is no victory without a fight.
Our minds we have to train and tame;
And have to abide by the rules of the game.
One false move and we are taken;
To our bits we are shaken.

But risks we need to take;
Because there is so much at stake,
And our future paths we have to make.
Sometimes, we do stumble and fall;
But we have to get up and give it our all.
Grit and determination and focus is what we need,
To surmount all our challenges and succeed.

Therefore we must be strong and grounded;
So that we don't get pounded.
For 'sweet' is the taste of success;
Even though it is not an easy process.
And the winner finally takes it all;
When with his' Victory Cup 'he stands tall.

An Ode to My Friends

Those were the days my friends
When our fun would never end
We were young and we were wild
And forever looked for ways to spice up our life

We were always happy and upbeat
And thought that the world was at our feet
There was no stopping our giggles
With whomsoever we mingled.

Each day brought a new song to our lips
And we loved to look hip .
Whether we wore red, blue or green
We were all in our fun loving teens

And we always sought for ways and means
To stop by for savouries and pastries at Flury's.
It was our favourite haunt
Where our styles we would flaunt

Be it Zeenat Aman, Parveen Babi or Hema Malini
We emulated each one of these heroines.
And we loved to strut down Park Street
In our high heeled clogs looking pretty and sweet.

Hostel food was bland and insipid
And we craved for ways to get a treat
Our day scholar friends were always very generous
With their home cooked brunches and luncheons.
And we always looked for ways to bunk our lectures
Because we thought that all our Professors were monsters

Ah...!! There is so much to gain
From going down memory lane
For it makes us feel youthful again
And imprinted in our hearts it will forever remain.

Desi Vibes

Bangles tinkling , and my Sari tucked in place
With a silver filigree brooch as always
No more high heels now , flat sandals will do
With a colourful bindi and a simple hairdo .
A single string of pearls and an elegant pair of diamond studs
Is all I need to complete my look .

It's always a traditional theme for the Ladies Sangeet
And I am looking forward to enjoying some desi beats .
Our big fat Indian weddings are the best
Where our dancing skills are put to test
And everyone dressed to kill
Despite running hefty bills.

The pretty young things shimmer in their glittering 'Jhumkas '
Gyrating to ..Pura London Thumakda ..with their' Thumkas'
And us oldies pitch in with our foot thumping too
As it makes us feel upbeat and good.

The bride makes a shy entry with her beau in tow
And amidst a sudden hushed silence , everyone stares in awe
As they dance in sync to mushy love songs without a flaw.

And the 'Masti' and fun continues from dusk to dawn
Till everyone gets exhausted and worn
But before I depart , the Mithai stalls are a must
As no Wedding is complete without the jalebis and gulab jamuns ..!!

Feelings

I sat by my window
Sipping my cup of tea
Lost in my thoughts of you
How great is this feeling
Of profound love...
It makes me want to skip and dance
And scream and shout
Under azure skies...
And feel the golden leaves
Crunch below my feet...
But alas, I am wheelchair bound
And I can only live it in my heart....!!!

The Yesteryears

Our lives were so simple, yet so cool
We didn't have TVs to stare at and drool.
Summer evenings were spent in the pool
And after that with homework from school
Sunday outings were always a treat
Either to the movies to beat the heat
Or with friends and family, a special meal.
Our Childhood fantasies came alive
With characters that in our minds did thrive
From story books that we devoured
And was the constant source of our delight.
Play time was always great fun
When we played Hide and seek and run
And of course the radio...the veritable jukebox
And the anthem of our lives...
That inevitably made us swing and jive.
To popular tunes of our time.
Slaves we have become now, of a digital world
Which we however can't do without
But our epitaphs we write even before our life unfurls.

The Dolphins

The dazzling blue waters of the ocean
Held my gaze hypnotically...
Whilst the sunlight played hide and seek
With the waves most capriciously.
And... from my deep contemplation
I was jolted instantaneously,
When, in a lightning, the sleek Dolphins flashed into my line of vision
As they leapt out of the waters in perfect unison
And nose dived back with absolute precision.

I was totally mesmerized to see such flawless synchronisation...
As I watched this captivating scene with rapt attention.
And felt so immersed in their joyous liberation.
Time stood still..
As they continued to add to my thrill.
And I couldn't get my fill..
Of their acrobatic skills.
I wanted to join them in their frolicking
And feel one with them by diving in..

Alas,... humans are bound by limitations.
But the limitless facets of nature's creations
Never fail to set me wondering
That without them, life
Would be so dull and boring
Their uninhibited antics is what makes our world so thrilling and exciting

You are not Alone

You are not alone
If life kicks you hard in your bones
And you cry softly on your own

You are not alone
If you have no one to rely upon
And you are on your own

You are not alone
When you search for memories
Within the folds of your diaries
And shed a tear or two
In remembering the ones dear to you

You are not alone if you have cried silent
tears at night
And wished for someone to hold you tight

You are not alone if you feel you are up
against the whole world
And you fight them for all your worth

You are not alone
If life throws bricks at you
And you don't know what to do

You are not alone if you are looking for love
and warmth
And live in the hope that it could help you tide over every
storm

You are not alone when you look for a silver
lining under every cloud
And feel optimistic and upbeat without a
doubt

And lastly you are not alone if you are
standing at the gateway of Heaven
Yet want to live life all over again.

Time Flies

Time flies by really fast
And before we know, our prime we have passed
So live every moment to the hilt
As if you were a king
Because youth fades and dies
In the twinkling of an eye.
Today here,...tomorrow no more.

But regrets we must harbour not
As, with our lives we can always do a lot.
Always strive to take the path less trod
For it will make your horizons more broad.
Aim high, for the skies
Because in you, your strength lies.
Trials and tribulations, you will face several;
But buckle under it,you should never.

There should be a fire in your soul
That must keep you on a roll.
Tap your potential
And make your credentials
And one day you will proudly stand and proclaim
I did it.....!!!..And now I have the fame..!!

The Peacock

I gasped in awe and delight
To behold this wondrous sight
As my feathered friend
Down the driveway did stride
In plumes so colourful and bright
An epitome of grace and dignity
And I marveled at nature's creativity
A sudden hop and onto the grass it went
To peck at the grains that were in a bowl laid
And then as if on cue
Its jewelled feathers were spread
In iridescent colours of every hue
A magnificent show of talent we did witness
In gay abandon it danced in our presence
And regaled us with its spectacular performance.
It is our national bird, there is no doubt
And it's not without reason, for it has the clout.

An Autumn Feast

The gust of wind blew the dried leaves across the lawn
Bespeckling the autumn grass freshly mown.
The maple trees stood shining with their golden halos
Displaying tinges of red, orange and yellow
Swishing and swaying madly in the breeze as if in a trance
Enjoying every moment of their joyful dance.
The sprightly squirrel darted quickly up the tree
To escape the fat, mean fox close at its heels
Who slunk away feeling cheated at the squirrel's cheek.

The prized, plump pumpkins lay at our feet
Waiting to be picked up for the festival of..Trick or Treat
And decorating them each year is such an enjoyable feat
As we sit on the sun deck deftly carving out scary faces
Between hot cups of tea and scrumptious sandwiches
And once completed, at the entrance verandah they will find a place
To regale and scare the visitors and our mates
And we all have a blast amidst this happy confusion
In trying to create a spooky atmosphere to befit the occasion.

A Slice of Life

Every morning when I look at myself in the mirror
I see a little bit of my old self disappear.
I no longer stand erect but am now bent in posture
And in my mind I get compelled to wonder,
That how, with the passage of time one changes forever.

Am I the same young girl who loved to dance ?
And always moved so gracefully as if in a trance ?
It feels like just yesterday, I was that young girl
Always happy to prance and twirl,
And amuse myself and regale everyone.
Always eager to try on a new dress
And to immaculate perfection get my hair dressed.

What I see now are deep furrows lining my face
Which I cannot erase.
But they are creases of a life well lived and faced
Of joys and laughter and tears, it is laced.
My hair has turned sparse and grey
And they tell their own tales.

Yet, I still long to dance
To be held in the arms of a man
And glide like a swan
To the rhythm of a special song
So each night in my dreams,
I step out to get transformed.

Anguish

The whole world is in a mess
Operating with total mindlessness.
No sooner did the fear of Corona vanish
Foolish mankind is back to being selfish.
Wars being waged, that are so senseless
Precious lives lost and so many made homeless.
And hapless victims rendered more helpless
By power hungry leaders who don't give a dime
Only wanting to get more ambitious with time.
Everywhere, communal hatred is running rife
And unleashing untold misery on human life.
The cries of dying babies and women rent the air
And there are bodies piled up everywhere.
People baying for each other's blood
And making a battleground of every neighborhood.
What a pity, these conflicts don't serve any purpose
Except giving rise to a generation scarred and very morose..

Desire

I encountered you in the by lanes of my emotions
And I felt elevated to great heights
As if buoyed on gigantic waves
Higher and higher I leapt
Embarking on an undeterred journey
Of joy and ecstasy
Disappearing behind the cottony mass of clouds
To play a game of love and seek
Did you compel me to drink some magic potion ?
That froze all my logical notions
Whilst you held me in your sway
At the same time keeping me at bay
In a torturous and tormenting way ?
Or do you revel in creating an air of mystery
And excel in concocting an enigmatic personality ?
You are all that I have ever hoped and longed for
And the intensity of my feelings should open up some door
To shake you out of your composure
So that you can be mine forevermore ..!

Sartorial Satan

One fine day, Satan raised his sartorial head
And beckoned me to hold his tempting hand
Into a bottomless chasm we descended
And down and down we spiralled
I saw sights I had never seen before
And felt emotions of deep allure
It was such a fascinating world
Of which I had never been a part of
My protected life I wanted to shake off
And taste the bitter sweet pangs of love
An intense desire took hold of me
As I succumbed to the one who led me
Heady scents numbed my senses
And I crossed the threshold of my fences
I was suffused with a feeling of pure ecstasy
The borders between sin and righteousness melted into fantasy
And I revelled in the grip of Satan's diabolical vagaries...

2022...The Year that was....!!

We are homeward bound at long last
All of twenty months our trip did last
The Covid scare kept us put
As travel worldwide on hold was put.

Everyone's lives it did throw out of gear
Stepping outdoors was never without fear
And as the pandemic raged and ravaged
Work from home became the rant.

An opportunity we got with our grandson to bond
A delight it was to watch and see him grow
From a Baby of eighteen months to a strapping 3 year old.
Smothering him with our love we did
As he is our very own dear little Sid.

And I am going to miss the pitter patter of his tiny feet
As he runs along the floor boards of polished teak
And his everyday cheerful wake up call to me
With a loud Good morning Dee..

The days were full of laughter and chatter
As he played with his toys and caused a lot of clutter
Every day, post dinner..a leg or two we shook

When on the floor of the living room we took
As Alexa complied to drive away our blues.

And I'm going to miss all this and much much more
For the Covid gave us all a chance to bond as never before.